# My Sundays with Normand

### ADÈLE FONTAINE

Tellwell Talent
www.tellwell.ca

ISBN
978-1-77370-788-4 (Paperback)

To you, Normand, because you loved us so deeply.

1937-2014

Death is so final
No more eating together
No more spending money
No more sharing things
No more discussions
No more laughter
No more cooking
No more writing
No more reading
No more listening to music
No more traveling together
No more, no more, no more
And all I want is more
More of you
Time is taking you away
And then I see you
Looking at me
From behind the Bose
Your hand resting on your cheek
Wearing your Ray-Bans
And my heart is pierced
In the silence
I feel the gentleness
Of the moment
Cut through the gloom
And suddenly
There is more
More flowers
More music
More words

_____

*January 10, 2015*

Each moment
That I live now
I greet you and smile
At the photographs
Placed
Around the house
I touch your face
And trace an outline
With my finger
Along the simple lines
Of your chin, your lips
And nose
Memorizing the shape and colour of your hair
In your eyes, the twinkle
I pick up one of your journals
And marvel
At your way with words
As I read the accounts
Of your life
I admire the artistic flourishes
You so lovingly engraved
Each symbol expressing what you held sacred
And so I weep
For my soul
Cannot contain
The vastness of you

———————————

*January 31, 2016*

I awaken to
A new day
A new year
Surrounded by silence
Outside the snow
Has made everything
Still
Another year
Without you
Last night we toasted
With champagne
Welcomed the New Year
With firecrackers
Dancing the night away
Somewhere in the music and song
You were there
As I settled down
For the night
I felt you
In the silence
Rising and falling
With each breath
I know
I can always
Find you
In the stillness
Of new days
And quiet nights

_____

*January 1, 2017*

We took down the tree
And left it outside
A few strings of popcorn
And cranberries
Left on the branches
Marie danced with it
Nathalie took pictures
And I stood there
Bringing to mind
The times
We brought the Christmas tree out
Planting it in a pile
Of snow
Sweeping up needles
Finding them later
On baseboards
And carpets
Standing where the tree
Had been
Holding each other
Remembering
Our children's pleasure
As they looked upon
The abundance
I hug myself
And reflect on the fullness
And wealth
Of all things
And how much I loved you

_____

*January 8, 2017*

And you are still gone
Never to return
Except in spirit
And that part of you
Is so vast
If I was an artist
A sculptor
A musician
Or a weaver
I would integrate
You in all my art
But no
I am a reader
A writer
A reciter of mantras
A seeker of truth
I keep searching for peace
I keep looking for you
Your death set my life ablaze
I am a house on fire
Everything
I touch burns
And every word I write
Brings light into this world

———————————

*January 22, 2017*

A small brown spider
Spins a web in our window
At first I think
It's a bit of dust
But no, it moves
Ignoring my grasping hand
As I watch
This tiny ball
Get back to its task
I wonder about
Things I see
And don't see
Things I hear
And don't hear
Things outside
And inside
Realizing that I am one
With all these things
And in that moment
Of quietness
I hear
A gentle voice
Say
Yes, *ma chérie*,
I too
Am one with all this

*January 21, 2018*

The sound this morning
Is white
Snow has been falling
Since Friday
Mud and grit
Underneath it all
One big-footed rabbit
Has left his presence
I stand and look
At the whiteness
And remember
All the snow
You shoveled
With a small white dog
At your side
When you came in to warm up
You'd stamp your feet
Smack your gloved hands
While puddles of wet snow
Gathered
On the floor
You'd taste the soup
Give me a hug
And a kiss
Open the door
And head out
Leaving me
With a blast of fresh air
And the warmth of your love

———————————

*January 28, 2018*

It's my birthday tomorrow
I know you would
Give me a great bouquet
Of pleasure and flowers
Then we would talk
Of our dreams and desires
Of our children
And their children
As we lay in bed
And let time slip away
In the warmth of our bodies
I know you would ask me
How I wanted my day to be
Was there anything else
I wanted
To make this a golden day
I could not imagine
Wanting anything more
Than being with you
I know you would tell me
That we could live
Without fear
Even though life is fragile
We'd hold each other
As we walked
Into the future

_____

*February 7, 2016*

Sometimes blackness
Surrounds me
Other times whiteness
And other times
Out of the blue
You come
Bearing gifts
Not tangible ones
That can be put on shelves
But gifts of light
Of pink skies
In the morning
Of bright sunny days
Of bird shapes
Made of snow
In nearby trees
Sometimes it is grayness
That covers me
Like a warm cloak
And sometimes purple
Owns me
Revealing the wound
Of sorrow and grief
The browns of time
Give me moments to walk
Back and forth
Through yellow wheat fields
You are still painting

———————————

*February 14, 2016*

I drove by
Our old house
This week
And the front porch
Light was on
You appeared
And asked gently
Would I like to go back
There was no doubt
In my mind
Yet I understood
That our time
On earth
Was gone
We have something else now
Undaunted spirits
Flying through days
Finding ways
To trust in goodness
As we hold on to reality
With our hearts and hands
With our words
And our songs

_____

*February 12, 2017*

I write to reveal
The unseen
In my world
To hold on to
The flashing
Images of you
I yearn to draw
A map
Of all the places
And things
We did
Is it you
I still hear
Or just my memory
Churning up thoughts
I have been
Unraveling our life
Thinking about
The what and where
Gently focusing
On endings
And slowly rolling
Them up
Into a ball
That I must use now
Before the fibers
Become thinner
And I become frailer

_February 19, 2017_

I've just finished reading
*Song of Batoche*
This is one
We would have read
Into the night
Discussing the details
It's about your heroes
Riel and Dumont
Such intense men
Louis so full of the Holy Spirit
Praying for God to be on his side
While Gabriel believed
The time for prayer
Was over
My head spins as I read
About the bloodshed
And defeat
When women had babies
As war waged around them
This event changed
The history of Canada
I shall never forget
What you did
In Ottawa
Looking at the statue of Macdonald
You slapped him across the face my darling
And said
This is for what you did
To Riel

———————————

*February 3, 2018*

I like to drive
Along the highway
With the radio on
And fill my belly with sound
And remember
How you surrounded
Us with music
To chase away
The days
When we felt overwhelmed
Bringing us the freedom
To see
That art and music
Were all that mattered
Where songs and melodies
Erased feelings of dread
With music and sound
We walked on clouds
Dancing our way
Through storms
And you my angel
Continue to reach out
With violins and guitars

---

*February 11, 2018*

There are still places
That cause me to tremble
And wonder
Could I have done more
Could I have been
More observant
Could I have been
More present
If I had loved you more
Would death
Have waited
And let you live
Longer
If the doctors
Had known
How to help
Would you still be here
These pointless
Questions, stirred up
By my grieving
Have no answers
And I love
How you simplify
*C'est ça qui est ça,*
*Pis y a rien qu'on peut faire*
I laugh and sigh
At your ruthless reality
Can I clear away the obstacles
Or find a place
To let go
Of the pain
I felt

As I watched
You dying
_____

*March 13, 2016*

It is the first of Spring
A day you loved
Walking
Barefoot
In the grass
Smelling the sap
Of your dear apple tree
You'd touch its small buds
And break the ice
In your prized water fountain
You'd walk through your garden
Scoop up some black earth
And promise
To fill it with seeds
When you saw your first robin
You'd make a wish
Now you are my Spring
The clouds I see
In the blue morning sky
You're the voice of the small chirping birds
The green in the grass
The buds on the trees
And the golden crowns of the daffodils
My bringer of change
Now a part of everything

———————————

*March 20, 2016*

You came to Costco with me
Put coffee cream and asparagus
into the shopping cart
I watched the packages
Slowly fall in
On the road towards home
I remember your trickster spirit
And weep
For sixteen months
I have mourned
And grieved
I no longer find words
To describe your absence
For you are still here
What right do I have to feel sad
Laughter fills our apartment
You lift your glasses and say
Give me your broken heart
So that I may restore it

———————————

*March 27, 2016*

A kind of disbelief
Comes over me
As I look at
Photographs of you
Your face
Your smile
Appear
Yet seem so far
Away
So long ago
Our lives so brief
Filled with work
Children
And friends
Books
Prayers
Delicious music
And sleep
So distant now
Like a stream
Where water once flowed
Yet somewhere
In the tall trees
A lone bird
Calls out
The spirit yes
But the flesh
Nevermore
Shall you see

———————————

*March 5, 2017*

As each day of the week passes
I pause and wonder
About our
Sunday meeting
I love this time
I've put aside
When I reach
Into infinity
And bring you back
This poetic journey
Takes me through
The life we lived together
I long to harvest the golden moments
The times when we loved
Unconditionally
With each verse
I compose
I cultivate
A new relationship
A covenant where
Our hearts intertwine
With the love that I find

---

*March 12, 2017*

I want to know
What life is like
In the world unseen
I know you watch
Over us
I feel
Your presence
When I fall asleep
And in the morning
When I wake
I wear your shoes
To feed the hungry birds
And rascally squirrels
You're there
When I bend and lace
My red boots
When I swim
In salt water pools
On Saturday afternoons
On my drive back home
Music plays on the radio
We used to share
The driver's seat
Now I listen to
Claude Saucier
As you fly
Through space
Your spirit
Sits by my side
From time to time

As I feel
My life shifting
To a new place

_____

*March 19, 2017*

I have learned to live
Without you
Yet there are times
When I so want you
To hear your signature honks
From the car
Where you sat waiting for us
With impatience for sure
But mostly joy
You never failed to knock
To let us know you were home
Two short knocks
And three in syncopated succession
You liked to tap out rhythms
As you listened to music
I'd give you the eye
If it got too loud
After dinner
You'd engage us
In a wine glass symphony
A few bars of
*Eine Kleine Nachtmusik*
Would fill the room
We'd applaud
And take our turns
Producing melodious sounds
My dearest maestro
I bow to you today

------------

*March 3, 2018*

The yard teams not with wildlife
But with sparrows, an old rabbit
And mounds of pure white snow
Too grainy to make a snowman
And still too much
For the middle of March
In my heart I long for spring
For the buzzing of bees
Hungry for nectar
In my heart
I yearn to see the grass
The crocuses, the irises
Yes, and even the dandelions and weeds
Reminding me to search
For my own greenery
You stand beside me
*Lâche pas*, you say
Ever encouraging me
To become the best
That I can be
Your death has brought me
To a place
Where words
Reveal
What is most sacred
I no longer fear the sting
Of chaotic emotions
I take only what I need

———————————

*March 11, 2018*

As I sit down
To spend time with you
Thoughts flash and flicker
As though I'm adjusting
The picture of an old TV
My brave darling
I call out
The colours are all wrong
Shut it off you say
And so I do
Come wander
Down the road
But I can't
I'm not ready
How do I keep
The promises we made
It's so hard to stay connected
I'm losing sight of you
These words I write each Sunday
Keep me close to you
Thus, are we united
One spirit, one human
Continuing their journey

———————————

*March 25, 2018*

I sit at our table
Me facing your empty chair
And remember our Sundays together
The words we unjumbled
The calls from our children
The laughter
The breakfasts we ate
The coffee you made
The birds at the window
The lilacs in bloom
I sit and remember the days
I spent with you

———————

*April 19, 2015*

Another Sunday
Without you
Feels bleak
Yet somewhere wonder
Sparks in me
As I consider
The mystery of our life
And my willingness
To keep
Asking questions
If we'd had more time
How different
Would each day have been
No different
You would say
*Puisque tous les jours*
*C'était fête*
*Et le plus simple déjeuner*
*Se transformait en banquet*
Your ability to marvel
A treasure
You brought me
From your childhood
That's it
It's wonder
That cracks open rocks
Wonder that makes life
Less raw
Wonder that helps us see
Life as it's meant to be

———————————

*April 3, 2016*

In my Easter photo
For this year
You are sitting
In the sun
Eating a popsicle
Surrounded by
Pansies and asters
Green grass
Spruce trees
80 feet high
A smile on your face
A mile wide
And this week in the news
Violence towards men
Women and children prevails
Outside snow
Covers the ground
There is too much
Darkness
Time to white out
The ugliness
Time to bring in
Love and sunshine

———————————

*April 16, 2016*

The candle burns
A turquoise colour
Folding and bending in on itself
On a yellow plate
I watch
As the day burns slowly away
Becoming a part of
The past, present and future
Why do I light
A candle
For my love
Who has left
It's more than
Just something to do
It keeps my attention
And helps me focus
On lightness
And silence
Opening a world
I had not imagined exists
Where nature reigns
The candle
Still burning
Welcomes me in

---

*April 19, 2016*

As I drive
Down the street
I look up
At the sky
A greyish cloud
Spreads out
Embracing
All that I am
I feel your presence
Cœur de pirate
Sings *Mistral gagnant*
And I feel
Your fingers
In the palm of my hand
And like you
I stay in the car
Lingering
Long after my arrival home
To hear the end
Of the song
We drive out
To Elk Island
Among the rolling hills
And hollows
I find you
In the trembling aspen
And white birch
I see your face
Your gentleness
Fills me with awe

At the wonders
That loving you
Has brought
And the north wind takes
It away

———————————

*April 2, 2017*

I really don't know
How to begin today
Maybe all I can do
Is take out your photo
And look at you
Or put on your housecoat
And sit around
All I know
Is that I want you
Here
Right now
In this yellow room
At the table
Sharing breakfast
I have no idea
What I would say
Just being with you
In the softness
Of the morning
Your body
Warm to my touch
Not cold and stone-like
Not ash
And then sharp and sudden
From the corner of my eye
I see you
Twirling like a dervish
Your action
Cuts through my longing
And joy bursts
Upon me

———————

*April 9, 2017*

Easter
Is not so easy
To describe
Snow has been falling
Far off
Spring is coming
The sky is
A whiter shade of blue
Someone has painted lines
With clouds
As I write
Words on white paper
Pale pink tulips
Slowly open
Celebrating Spring
And I in this
Budding country
Seek light
Somewhere in those simple pleasures
I listen for your footsteps
Look for
A surprise
Do you remember the chocolate eggs
You loved to hide
A memory comes
Just in time
You and I standing
In the sun
Licking popsicles
A perfect Eastertime

---

*April 16, 2017*

Come see the yard
All covered in snow
As I look out
This morning
I hold my breath
Knowing you would
Have something to say
You who wrote about weather
Who talked about it
Who treated weather
As a gift
A package
To be opened and examined
I stand at the open door
A brown rabbit sits
By the poplar tree
The swing on the deck
Sways gently
And the sky
White as the ground
Dares me
To find you
On this cold day
In the distance
I hear geese
Wind
Water flowing
Something moves
On the flower bed
A crocus is pushing
Its way to the sun

_____

*April 23, 2017*

The powdery snow
That fell last night
Made the snowdrifts
Look like Stollen
A yard
Full of bread
Good bread
Not stolen
Given freely
Like manna
I can see you
Orchestrating
This wonderful banquet
Can you imagine
Slicing and serving it
Can you imagine
The self-serving people
Suddenly awaking
Can you imagine
The taste
And the satisfaction
Where could I go
For such a delicacy
A gentle wind
Reminds me
Of Geshela
My Buddhist teacher
Train your mind
He would say
It is everything

---

*April 1, 2018*

Spring is still far away
Dried brown leaves
Are falling
In the snow
I have no idea
What season this is
Birds empty the feeder
As quickly as it is filled
Friends post photos
Of crocuses
From other springs
A few things are certain
Taxes must be paid
Georges Dor and Andy Williams
Will always sing
My favorite love songs
I can still drive
Down the highway
Listening to the radio
Full-blast
Remembering
The two of us
Holding hands
The doctor calling us together
I'll sit beside you
He softly said
Because he's yours

_____

*April 8, 2018*

I walk in sadness
Knowing I must find
The happiness I seek
I'm the creator of my dreams
The maker of my thoughts
How do I shake the heaviness
How do I wash it out
It keeps weighing me down
Each time I bend my head
I cannot lift it
Your death
Holds me in its grasp
Yet I stay on the path
Of letting go

———————————

*May 3, 2015*

What will today bring
I wonder
As I start
My Sunday poem
I hear you clearly say
I am near
Find me
In the flame of the candle
In the bouquet of peonies
You are everywhere
Even in your absence
I hear
Your laughter
Your bare feet on the floor
I feel your arms holding me
Whispering
Happy Mother's Day
Sadness
Fills the room
As another town
Burns to the ground
I witness
Your joy as you watch
The birds
The trees
The flowers
The clouds and the sky
I know you would love
This place in the dales
So close to the river
Let me tell you one thing
My dear
You are worth every minute

I grieve
Every moment I mourn
Because you are mine
Normand Fontaine

_____

*May 8, 2016*

I am slowly learning
That death changes
Everything
Death is like
A mirror
We can see
But never touch
We can remember
But never keep
Moments we shared
Are like negatives
I must bring them
Into the light
Before they fade
I'm standing
At the window
You are by my side
As we look at the garden
The apple and plum trees
Are in bloom
You planted marigolds
Neatly in a row
We breathe in
The fragrant scent of
Thérèse Bugnets
Anticipate the bounty
From our raspberry bushes
I reach for your hand
But you are gone
I see our life together
As I recall the things we did
Still full of meaning

I take the hoe
And watering can
And go out to plant geraniums

_____

*May 15, 2016*

The chit-chat of the birds
At dawn
Your favorite morning alarm
On the candle
Of the pine tree
A robin sings
I ask the birds
On this fine day
To tell me what they've learned
Stay calm
The chickadee says
As it eats from
My hand
Find joy and delight
The blue-jay screeches
When it finds the nuts
I placed on the fence
Let go of your anger
The magpie urges
It will only hold you back
Experience the wonder
The nighthawk cries
As it loops through the evening skies
Be grateful says
The northern flicker
As it pecks at the cake
Made of berries and suet
These birds you loved so dearly
Are my friends now

———————

*May 7, 2017*

You were not afraid
To pray
The mantras
You chose
Resonated
In your mind
And in your body
You wrote them
On paintings
Wove them on
Pillowcases and bedclothes
Traced them
In snow
And dust
Your god
Your buddha
Was a woman
Who wept
Who laughed
Who loved humanity
You believed
Heaven and hell
Were in the here and the now
Your place of worship
Was in the natural world
Today I see you everywhere
In bumblebees
And flowers

Your manifestations
Keep me grounded
In this bright
Yet broken world

_____

*May 14, 2017*

You loved our apple tree
Its buds and boughs
Its delicate white flowers
Which made the air
Smell so sweet
Its five varieties
Of fruit
Provided food
And shelter to birds
You loved our apple tree
It held
The most beautiful parts
Of life
Contentment and strength
Light and shadow
The ability to change
And then one day
Early in the fall
I cut it down
I couldn't stand
The mess it made
The way the branches
Poked in the sky
The rotting fruit
The fallen leaves
And you my darling
When you came out
Stood
In horror
And wept

---

*May 21, 2017*

Morning again
And you're still not here
Where are you
My heart asks
Yet hates knowing the answer
I miss hearing your voice
And laughter
The hole in my heart
Longs for you
You who
Made my life so sweet
Always found
Joy among the days
I cannot imagine myself without you
I put on your gardening shoes
And go out to check on the birds
And remember
You saying
They were not the best for walking
But maybe they're the best
For feeding birds

_____

*June 9, 2015*

In the river
Of no return
I try to stay protected
The shore is safe
Water surrounds me
And pulls me
To the center
Your spirit
Urges me to continue
The journey
Of grief
It's Father's Day
A time to celebrate
The lives
We created
With each other
I reach
For your hand
My broken heart
Says
Let go
Live on
Let the waves of light
And compassion
Lead you
To another day

---

*June 21, 2015*

I can't describe
What's happening to me
Even breathing
Is difficult
Is missing someone
Real
Is losing you
Going to feel like forever
Is describing
This grief
Possible
I can no longer
Stand
Being without you
I long for you
And yet I know
Your death
Was real
We lost you
All of us
Did it hurt you
To leave
Because not having you
Aches so badly
When I see images of your face
On walls
It's not your picture I crave
It's you
Goddammit

———————

*June 29, 2015*

Five years ago
Claude Lévéillée died
We spent the day
Listening to his songs
We cooked a delicious meal
And drank a bottle
Of Le Grand Vin
For 53 years
We fell in and out of love
Changed our sheets
Spent time in bed
Went on holidays
Invited family and friends
Did laundry
Ate, walked
Dreamed and slept
Mowed the lawn
Planned renovations
Spent money
Beautified our yard
Watered the garden
Washed windows
Dusted and cleaned
Often just in silence
We did jumbles together
Left notes for one another
Watched television
*Toujours les postes français*
Spoke to our children
In Germany, Ottawa
and Montréal
We did 10-minute writings

I read, you journaled
I read, you painted
Remembrance
Brings me face-to-face
With the young woman
Who found love in you

_____

*June 5, 2016*

Let's cross the bridge today
Which one I ask
The one that's in your heart
Oh, that's too long
Who knows what's
On the other side
Ah
You say
But there is no other way
Alright let's go find her
That spunky girl
I used to be
The one who lied
Who ate too much cake
Who smoked and spent
All our money
Who liked to drink wine and flirt
Who cheated
Fiercely sometimes
Yes, her
That wild being you once were
I want her back
She was more than
I deserved
A gift totally unexpected
She's all yours now

———————

*June 19, 2016*

I dreamt of you
On Thursday night
You came walking down
the road
And oh!
The joy I felt
I went to hold you
You said, no
I'm much too fragile
I noticed your body
Was made of dust
A mix of grays
And streaks of gold
Perfectly formed
I looked and looked
Satisfying my hunger
Knowing how much
I loved you
We sat and spoke
I can't stay, you said
I have many people to see
But come with me
A bit of the way
We got into a truck
As blue as the sky
I laughed watching you
Turning the wheel
A little side to side
You dropped me off
On the corner of a cloud
We waved goodbye

And I watched as your body
Dissolved into stardust

———————

*June 11, 2017*

Last July
You were still here
Doing jumbles
And drinking fresh coffee
What was the weather like
*Pas d'ouragan*
*Pas d'inondation*
*Pas de présence militaire dans ma rue*
How long would you live
You thought till 2027
Ninety years
Would be good
At two in the morning
An electric storm
Illuminated the neighborhood
You woke me up
To come and see it
The last movie we saw together
*Dawn of the Planet of the Apes*
You marveled at Matt Reeves' talent
And oh
How your knees and legs
Caused you much pain
How will we spend
Our anniversary
You wondered
We walked
Towards our destiny
Not knowing
You had five months left

———————

*July 5, 2015*

My life is changing
Minute by minute
Causing me to ponder
Which is more powerful
Life or death
How do I navigate
The waters of impermanence
Death changes
How life is lived
How I view
The suffering of others
I wonder
What part of me longs
Most for you
My eyes
My ears
My hands
My feet
Or my heart

---

*July 3, 2016*

You are my Edmonton
Yet there are
Places
I can't go
Vi's Café for shepherd's pie
The Blue Plate for onion cakes
Deep fried wontons at Bulgogi
I hear you say
If we decide on
A place
That's where we'll go
And you can't
Change your mind
And oh, how my eyes
Would go ballistic
I realize now
It was a joke
And I took you
So seriously
It's these moments
I miss
Because you knew
How to play
All the strings
Of my heart

_____

*July 18, 2016*

I need to share
With you some truths
About our family
Not one of us is perfect
Our journeys fraught
With fear and trembling
It is in that knowing
That we find the courage
To connect
And hold our vulnerability
As a shield
Nothing more
We struggle to find
A sense of belonging
Often hurting each other
As we learn
To travel lighter
Blaming and hating
Wanting so much
To be considered kind
And loving
We shudder
As we discover
The shadow side of ourselves
The bossy little emperors
The sickly-sweet sycophants
I know you laugh
And love us even more
And we so full of ego
Must learn to release
And let go

_____

*July 31, 2016*

One of your favorite
Musician's was Bach
He brought you great joy
You said
He expressed
The inexpressible
You listened to his music
In every form
You didn't grow up
Listening to Bach
It was Jimmy Rogers
Hank Snow and the Carters
In your adolescence
You discovered
Classical music
Your life work
As a radio announcer
Allowed you to serve
Your listeners
Cantatas and concertos
One day
You told me
That Bach had composed
A cantata each Sunday
For his Lutheran congregation
And now week in
And week out
Since your death
I too write
Cantatas for you

———————

*July 17, 2017*

The morning sun
Warms the yard
Small birds run
Across the fence
Geraniums in blue pots
Rose hips on branches
And my heart
Calls out to you
Do you recall
How we spent
Our summer vacations
On beaches
And cottages
At so many different lakes
Could it be that
We became parents
Of seven children
Within ten summers
How did we do it
Was it the music
The dance
Or the wine
I think it was
Because
We were good friends

———————————

*July 30, 2017*

I feel the silence
In our house
The silence in your room
The silence at the table
The silence in the sunroom
In the stairs
In the car
But then the radio
Which you loved
Blasts out some French rap
I change the station
And le grand Alain Bashung
Sings *Un jour viendra*
I turn to you
We weep
A thing we always did
When we heard him
Now we both know
That day has come
And one of us is gone
Nine months have passed
Did we love enough
Did we fight fair
Did we hate each other sometimes
Yes, we both answer
With tears streaking down our faces

———————————

*August 30, 2015*

Early this morning
I dream about peeling oranges
I know it'll make a mess
Hopefully this one
Has a lot of pith
If only you were here
You'd slice off the top
And bottom
Crack the line
Down the middle
And open it
Like an accordion
Eating the juice filled sacs
This orange is different
The pithy peel
sticks under my nails
The more I take off
The more there is
I love
The inside
Of the peel
I finish the orange
And find a small
Golden seed

_____

*August 21, 2016*

Mist hangs over the yard
And through the trees
The sun shines bright
I think of all the mornings
We witnessed together
I find your journal
Of August 6, 2007
We were in Jasper
Mist covers
Roche Bonhomme
With the sun
Brilliant as ever
We hike
The trails around
Maligne Lake
Breathing deeply
As our children
And their children
Run ahead
We name the flowers
Along the path
Blue flax
And Brown-eyed Susans
As well the trees and the birds
In the distance
We see Spirit Island
And in that moment
I know
We will always be

―――――――――――

*August 6, 2017*

How do we walk
With love
By leaping
Into spacious sky
Dragging roots
Of all that is
Learning
To embrace
And not faint
At ugly
Witnessing
The edges
Of beauty
Swimming in it
Laughing in it
Traveling in the front seat
Never letting go
Graciously
Growing old
Reinventing
Exploring
I hear you say
Don't be afraid
Of loving too much

---

*August 26, 2017*

It's been too many days
Too many nights
This loss of you
Has become too much
Grieving is a country
A planet, a universe
Yet I must learn to inhabit
This unbeautiful place
Where can I find
The road
Back to life
*Cherche la beauté*
*De chaque instant*
*Tu me dis en souriant*
Are you mocking me
I want to scream
The ground
Disappears
Turns into an ocean
The moon rises
As you leap into the sky

――――――――

*Sept. 13, 2015*

Adèle Fontaine

I moved yesterday
To this new home
There's a place for everything
You brought into my life
Your art, your music
Your journals and birds
In this community
I know I will
Keep finding you
In the people
The trees and the river
I know when our children
Come
They too will find you here
I need you to help me
Use the past
To shape my present and future
*Notre premier visiteur*
*Sascha*
*M'apporte la bouilloire*
*Et du thé*
I place your ashes
Where the stereo
Used to be
Wondering when
We will gather
To let them go

---

*September 20, 2015*

How do I begin
Another day
With a few words
At the top of the page
I kept your blue housecoat
And wondered where to put it
As I held it
In my hands
A passing parade of mornings
Came to mind
Barefoot
In the snow
Your housecoat
Wrapped tightly around you
You stepped out
To get the paper
You flashed me
As I came down the stairs
I rushed into your arms
And leaned into your warm body
A perfect beginning to our day

_____

*September 27, 2015*

A handful of words
A heart full of love
More than enough
The hidden power
Revealed
In the promise
We made
To never lose touch
Little did I know
That every Sunday
We would have
Deep conversations
Little did I know
Our joy
Of playing with words
And making sentences
Would be the way
I'd find you
Little did I know
This ritual
Would create
Such extraordinary
Moments

———————————

*September 3, 2017*

As I consider
All the days
We spent
Together
I realize
The past
Does not lie still
Or fade into
A distant memory
It builds upon
Each day
Shifting
And changing
You are my sacred witness
Abiding within
And without
Understanding
That I must remove
The bandages
Wrapped around
My broken heart

---

*September 17, 2017*

Come scream
With me today
About death
And the loss of my sister's
Beloved daughter
Imagine her
Rocking her body
Sifting
Through pictures
Of her smiling child
Listen to her
As she tells stories
About drugs and addiction
And wonder
How best to honour
Her daughter's gifts
Come pray with me
Sending waves
Of compassionate love
As she grieves
With her family
Come walk
With me today
See how autumn
Has changed
The colour
Of the river valley
See the magpies and crows
Perched on power lines

Notice the scraggly
Red poppies
The powder grey sky

_____

*September 24, 2017*

I have hung up
Some of your paintings
Creativity and imagination
Now reign in this place
Forests and trees
Marching insects
Embossed in gold
Small pink stars
Blue skies
Yellows
Greys, whites and reds
Lines, forms and figures
Bend and stretch
Everything is connected
Your passion for small things
Each shape
Unknown
Until you set it
On a canvas
An ocean
Within a golden frame
A winter scene
With dear Old Floss
Prairies, mountains
And rolling hills
You created your own universe
On so many paintings
You honoured
The shack
Your precious childhood home
Yet feared the eyes
Of the heartless observer

Oh, my dearest
You have left me with
Uncountable treasures

_____

*October 11, 2015*

Eleven months ago
You died
And left us
To weep and grieve
Now you are
In everything we see
Yesterday as Marie and I
Read one of your journals
We longed for you
You left us far too soon
You had words
To write
Songs to play
A garden to tend
Birds to feed
Thoughts to express
Love to give
Jokes to tell
Letters to write
Paintings to paint
My darling Normand
You inspired us
In so many ways
To add to the world
You helped create

---

*October 25, 2015*

I've been thinking
About you
And wondering
How you experienced
Your last months
On earth
You whisper softly in my ear
Except for
You all being there
Nothing was good anymore
Sensors, ventilators
Catheters and electrodes
Kept my body alive
As I slowly let go
Of the life I knew
You held my hands
And with fragrant ointments
Massaged my feet and belly
You debated
With the critical care team
Of doctors and nurses
You danced and fed me oranges
You offered me
Stories and songs
With my mind intact
I witnessed
Your loving kindness
And was ready
To move on

_____

*October 2, 2016*

A white sheet
Flutters in the wind
On a computer screen
A rectangle
Changes
Into a page
A woman
Walks up a hill
Alone
A crow sits
On a pole
Above her head
A jet
Leaves a trail
And from pale brown grass
A faint odor
Of earth
Brings images
Of warmth
A man
Sits by a fireplace
Chewing his lip
Strokes
A small dog
While Bach's *Adagio in D Minor*
Fills the room
Someone calls
From an open window
It's time to go forward
A new adventure
Awaits

---

*October 23, 2016*

I awaken
This morning
To the sweet song
Of a green bird
On a branch
A glimpse only
And he is gone
Yet the image
Lingers
In my mind
The greenness
Of the feathers
The wee yellow feet
The full-throated song
Calling my spirit back
Silently I walk
Through the house
Touching your paintings
And am filled with gladness

———————————

*October 22, 2017*

Three years ago
You could
Still hold my hand
Still smile and respond
To music
To pain
You were alive
Yet you were coming
To the end
You wondered
About the power
Of your spirit
Would it
Manifest itself
As a wolf or coyote
Or a whistling wind
Knowing you, you'd
Want to try your hand
At being everything
Leaves, grass, clouds, songs
And I know you're even a part
Of flowing water

———————————

*October 29, 2017*

I want to create a space
Where I can hold you
But like the weather
Everything keeps changing
I see you fly off
On a horse-shaped cloud
With a wink and a smile
You leave me
Yearning
For your warmth
It's as though I am water
And have become one
With sadness
And yet
My beating heart
Dares me to live

_____

*November 8, 2015*

If I had to describe
What missing you
Feels like
I'd cast off
From the shore
Of gratitude
To settle in a place
Where longing dwells
Where the ache
That penetrates my whole body
Seeks to reach
Out and bring you back
No joy resides here
I try to express
My love for you
But my darling
You are nowhere to be found
In this place I even miss our disagreements
Missing you
Requires strength
And untold power
And yet
I would never
Seek immunity

———————————

*November 20, 2016*

November is
The month of your birth
The month of your death
The month when we miss
You most
November meant
Frosty morning hikes
And family visits up north
When November comes
We wonder if you're
Up there
In the stars
Or hiding behind a passing cloud
On your birthday
We buy flowers
Light candles
Make delicious food and cake
As though you were with us
To celebrate
Because maybe love
Is stronger than death

_____

*November 5, 2017*

We lit a bright red candle
In the early morn
At first the flame
Attempted to leap
Off the wick
Then it flickered gently
Upwards
Leaving no shadow
Outside on this cold and wintery day
Black-capped chickadees
Redpolls and downy woodpeckers
Snacked on seeds and suet
Inside by the fire
We played music
Told stories
Made gingerbread cake
Jacob blew out your birthday candles
Together we sang
*Mon cher Normand*
And knew
Your spirit
Was with us still

---

*November 12, 2017*

When I drive
You're with me
Not in the passenger's seat
But on the radio
Cuing the disc
Back spinning
Announcing the artist
Describing their music
With your playful voice
You hum to Frank Mills
*Music Box Dancer*
And sing along
With Gainsbourg
*69 année érotique*
The music fades
Another song
One of your favorites
Georges Dor
*Si tu savais*
*Comme on s'ennuie*

_____

*November 19, 2017*

You woke me this morning
Saying
Come
It's time to write about us
For that is when your words
Become flesh
When you pan
For the gold
Of 53 years
Shared together
How can I write
About this
Without falling apart
I wonder
As my tears
Blur the page
How can I look at the past
When the present is still so raw
How can the right words
find me
When all that is left
Are your ashes
*Ben voyons, tu me dis*
*Prends ton courage*
*À deux mains*
*Pis vas-y*
I remember you saying
Something like this
As I gave birth
To each of our seven children

Not knowing
Mourning
The most difficult of tasks
Lay ahead

_____

*December 13, 2015*

On Wednesday morning
I burnt the oatmeal
And set off the alarm
The pot was black
I thought I'd better
Toss it
But then I saw you
Roll up your sleeves
It was a WearEver pot after all
A saucepan my mother had bought
From a traveling salesman
We'd cooked and burnt
Many sauces and soups in it
And you'd rush in like a knight to clean it
So I scoured
Thinking of the wealth
Of sugar and butter
We'd feasted upon
I rinsed it and smiled
This aluminum object
You so diligently scrubbed
Was now my pot of gold

---

*December 11, 2016*

If I wanted to write
A love song
I would ask
Whether love has a form
Does it dwell
Deep within
Or float
On the surface
If I wrote
A love song
I'd follow one rule
There would have to be death
Because love is
Always transcending
If I could cut through
The chaos
That lies
At the heart
Of everything
Yes, maybe then
I could write
A love song
You could
Whistle and hum
And I'd gladly dance alone

--------------------

*December 18, 2016*

It's Sunday
And just before I wake
You walk
Into my room
It's time to write
Time to connect
As my thoughts unfold
I remember
You and I agreeing
That everything
Was sacred
Full of mystery
That we would never accept
Too small a reality
I loved how we opened
Ourselves wide
To embrace all that came

_____

*December 3, 2017*

Christmas is around
The corner
So much work to do
In preparing
For the holiday season
This festive celebration
Changed
When our children left
We created new rituals
Invited others to our home
Now the most difficult task
My darling
Is having Christmas
Without you
On a leafless branch
A single bird chirps
I stretch out
My arms
To embrace
The cold, snowy days
Of another winter alone

———————————

*Dec 17, 2017*

I find it hard to describe
The mystery of winter
It starts with the shortest day
And the longest night
A radiant sun
That rises later
And holds its place
A golden shawl
Spreading across the sky
In the fresh
Fallen snow
I see footprints
Who could have
Walked here
I wonder
As a small breeze
Brushes against my lips

———————————

*December 24, 2017*

# Afterword

*by Danielle Fontaine*

It was when Papa died
We hated that day
We would rather anything than that
To lose our best
Papa
Who warmed our hands and toes with his breath
Who taught us the love of music and birds and small incidental
things no one notices
He most gentle and forgiving
He was the one who was supposed to win
Some battle with open heart
We raged
We wailed
Our mom
She did
What she often did
She wondered if she was bereaved or bereft
We gathered together
And then we left her for our various corners
She looked at all the beauty that was her life with dad
She held it in her hands like so many sparkling pebbles
She let the pebbles fall like water
She sold the house
Framed his art
Saved and read his journals
Full of perfect cursive
Held his ashes for one year
And then let them go

We were transformed
We could feel him still blooming
Inside our hearts
Like a new strange, invisible and magical flower
Mom fashioned a new life
She walked with this daily loss
But decided
Like she always does
To create
She began her Sunday devotions
Her Sunday poems for dad
Every time Sunday comes
I look forward with joy and apprehension
I read a new one and it is like
Opening a gift
Discovering a new bird
Hearing a new song
Finding a new colour

_____

*February 11, 2018*

# Acknowledgements

I would like to thank my family and friends for encouraging me with their love and support.

A special thanks to Susan, Reinhild, Valary and Jocelyne for helping me to believe in life after death.

And finally, to my dear editor and roommate Marie Fontaine for helping me bring musicality to my poetry.

Made in the USA
Lexington, KY
28 August 2019